The Laying on of Hands and Anointing

in Ministry for Wholeness and Healing

Carolyn Headley

Tutor in Liturgy, Wycliffe Hall, Oxford

GROVE BOOKS LIMITED
RIDLEY HALL RD CAMBRIDGE CB3 9HU

Contents

Acknowledgments

The original piece of college work, from which the first booklet on this subject stemmed, owed a great deal to those who supervised and encouraged my study. Among these I continue to thank Bishop Morris Maddocks, Canon David Wheaton, David Field and Brigid Pailthorpe. Since then there have been many who have contributed to my understanding of this subject, notably the people of the parishes of Kensal Rise, in Harlesden, London, and of Uxbridge, in Middlesex. More recently the staff and students of Wycliffe Hall, and the other members of GROW, have all continued to stimulate thinking and to challenge my assumptions. John Leach, James Steven and Anna de Lange have been kind enough to read this booklet and make helpful comments.

The Cover Illustration is by Peter Ashton and Janet Rimmer

First Impression October 2002
ISSN 0144-1728
ISBN 1 85174 511 4

Introduction

1

The ministry of wholeness and healing is increasingly part of the life of local churches.

The report *A Time to Heal* and liturgical provision in the *Common Worship Pastoral Services*[1] will give further impetus to the ministry of wholeness and healing, at a time when there is such need for it in a broken and fragmented world. This new edition of the original 1988 booklet is being published to provide a practical Grove handbook to the CW services. Although a substantial amount of the material remains unchanged, several new areas are included. The ministry has been steadily extending into many congregations over the last two decades, and alongside this the 'Third Wave' of renewal since the 1980s has directly or indirectly affected churches of all denominations. There is increased willingness by church leaders to share the ministry with the whole church so that vast numbers of Christians are now engaged in this work and witness of the kingdom. These developments have prompted some additional sections, and in a general reworking I have tried to make the booklet more practically useful. It is only a brief introduction to a vast subject, and in no way aims to be a comprehensive treatment, and it focusses specifically on the laying on of hands and anointing.

Vast numbers of Christians are now engaged in this work and witness of the kingdom

My background as a physiotherapist, engaged in the healing ministry of the church, brought together medical and theological thinking. My experience was of seeing God at work in both the hospital and the local congregation, and touch played a major part in the ministry of both. Touch is in itself beneficial physically, psychologically and socially. Through Christ, and by the Holy Spirit, it also communicates God's love, and becomes Christ's own touch in the ministry of his church.

By the Holy Spirit, touch communicates God's love and becomes Christ's own touch

2   The Biblical Background

Old Testament Background

Prayer for 'healing' needs to be made with an understanding of what true 'health' actually is, and that begins with the biblical concept of wholeness.

God's promise of wholeness and healing in the Old Testament centres around the possibility of a health-giving set of relationships. A right relationship with God, with oneself, with the family, with the community, and with the world around results in *shalom*. As part of the covenant God lays down laws for his people that will enable good living in these terms, and the Ten Commandments reflect this holistic approach to life and health. By keeping the commandments God's people will 'enjoy long life,' 'so that it may go well with [them] and that [they] may increase greatly in a land flowing with milk and honey' (Deuteronomy 6.1–3, 17–18). God wanted harmony and well-being for his people at every level, and *shalom* comes about whenever God's will is being done. It has community, religious and personal implications.

> *God wanted harmony and well-being for his people at every level*

But the fallen nature of humankind leads more to disobedience and discord than to obedience and harmony, resulting in dis-ease and various forms of dysfunctional suffering. So although healing is mentioned frequently in the Old Testament, it is mainly in the context of reward for obedience, as disease was judgment for disobedience. Healing is seen in its broadest sense as the restoration of *shalom*, with the predominant idea of the healing of the nation rather than of individuals. It is on return to God's will that healing is promised in frequent calls to repent (for example 2 Chr 7.14; Hosea 14.1–4; Jer 3.22). Atonement for sin will therefore also bring healing as seen in the Suffering Servant passage in Isaiah 53.4–5.

> *Healing is in God's nature: 'I am the God who heals you'*

It follows that health and healing are signs of God's blessing, especially when the nation has the role of witnessing to God's power and glory. Individual healing is not often recorded except as it affects the story of God's dealing with his people, or to authenticate ministry, as with Moses, Elijah and Elisha, or to demonstrate God's power over pagan gods.

Healing is in God's nature, as is shown by the title he gives to himself when speaking to Moses—'I am the God who heals you' (or 'your Healer,' Exodus 15.26), but it is within this clear context of covenantal relationship and with more of a corporate than an individual emphasis.

The Laying on of Hands and Anointing in the OT

The laying on of hands was used for designating a person or an object to some specific purpose for God.

It was used for blessing, commissioning, dedication, and consecration. There are two words used for imposition of hands—*samak*, and *sît* or *sîm*.

- *samak* means to lean or rest upon. So this laying on of hands has force and weight behind it. The pressure carries a sense of trans-ference—'putting upon.' The commissioning of Joshua, making him Moses' substitute, entailed putting upon him something of Moses' personality and gifts for God's service. The same word is used in the dedication of Levites by the congregation, for sins be-ing put upon a scapegoat, for leaning on an animal to be sacrificed, and for putting back onto someone accused of blasphemy any taint or associated guilt before execution.

- *sît* and *sîm* are general, interchangeable, words for putting and placing. In relation to placing hands upon, they are used most in the sense of blessing, as in Jacob's blessing of his sons, and (linked to healing) when Elisha placed his hands on the child's hands to revive him. They carry the idea of transfer of influence, but not the heavy touch of leaning upon and putting upon that *samak* carries.

The distinction in Hebrew between these two different forms of imposition of hands is lost in the Septuagint. However, by New Testament times rab-binic literature shows the distinction regained, with the practice of *samak* being restricted to the sacrificial cult and the ordination of rabbis.

Two other words for touch are related to healing. *marach* is used, for exam-ple, in the instruction to rub Hezekiah's boil with a cake of figs (Isaiah 38.21). And *naga'* is a word for coming into contact, as used in laws related to clean-liness, and for reaching out or striking (including striking by a disease). Neither refer to the laying on of hands as such.

In the few Old Testament instances of individual healing, various physical acts other than the laying on of hands were involved. The nearest to it is Elijah and Elisha stretching over the children's bodies (1 Kings 17.21–22, 2 Kings 4.32f).

Anointing was used to designate, consecrate and sanctify objects and people for God's purposes in the Old Testament. Three key passages will serve to illustrate this, although there are multiple references to its use. Exodus 29–30 and Leviticus 8 describe how Aaron and his descendants, and their priestly garments, were to be anointed. A recipe is given for the making of the 'holy anointing oil,' which was also to be used to consecrate other articles designated as holy. 1 Samuel 16.1–13 describes the anointing of David by Samuel, designating him as God's choice as king, and from that day the Spirit of the Lord came on David in power. It was similarly used in the crowning of kings. Anointing marked, or even effected, such a close association with God that the anointed one is identified with God himself, and carries his authority.

With regard to healing, the medicinal use of oil was widely accepted throughout the ancient near east, and this is reflected in the Old Testament. Its nourishing ability strengthens and confers well-being, and its soothing, healing properties lead to its use in a symbolic way related to restoration after illness, or an end to mourning. For example, there was a ceremony for someone free of infectious skin disease which marked an end to their exclusion from the community (Leviticus 14.14–18). Jesus presumably expected the healed lepers to receive this when he sent them to the priest (Matthew 8.4 and Luke 17.14). Oil was also used in celebrations and weddings.

So the concept of the promised Messiah as the Anointed One has the background of priestly and royal anointing, associations of consecration, healing and celebration of life and identification with Almighty God.

New Testament Background

Jesus came to establish God's rule and kingdom in fulfilment of the Old Testament hope and promise (Luke 4.18–19 and 7.22, echoing Isaiah 61.1–2, 29.18–19 and 35.5–6). With Jesus there is healing at all levels and in all spheres of creation, bringing in the new age, and proclaiming God's kingdom in word and deed. Healing is the re-establishing of the lost *shalom*, although it will only finally be realized in death as our eternal life, in him and through him, is fulfilled.

With Jesus there is healing at all levels and in all spheres of creation

When Jesus sent out the twelve and the seventy, he sent them to preach and to heal, to continue his work of proclaiming the kingdom, demonstrating it in signs and wonders. The ministry begun by Jesus was bequeathed to the church, equipped by the Holy Spirit.

In Acts the references to healing seem to be symbolic episodes. If plotted on a map, they show salvation and healing going hand in hand. The gospel spreads from Jerusalem (Acts 3–4, 5.12–16) to Samaria (8.4–13), Damascus (9.3–25), Lydda (9.32–35), Joppa (9.36–41), Lystra (14.8–10, 19–20), Philippi (16.16–18), Ephesus (19.11–12), Troas (20.7–12) and to Malta (28.1–10). This recording of significant points of growth demonstrates how the risen Christ was present, and his authority evident, as the disciples responded to the great commission (Matt 28.30). His power was at work in them and through them as they witnessed to him in Jerusalem, and in all Judea and Samaria, and to the ends of the earth (Acts 1.8). As well as these specific recorded incidents we see in the epistles that healing was seen as one of the *charismata* or gifts given to the whole body of Christ (1 Cor 12–14).

Healing was seen as one of the 'charismata' given to the whole body of Christ

James again underlines the total healing, physical and spiritual, that the Lord gives through his church. In 5.13–16 the writer uses three words (and implies a fourth) for sickness, or suffering, and a whole range of words for their healing: *kakopathei* (v 13) for the suffering of those who were persecuted, troubled, afflicted or in difficulty; *asthenei* (v 14) for weakness and infirmity; and *kamnonta* (v 15) with the sense of being worn out or exhausted, possibly referring to geriatrics or those approaching death. Implied in 15b and 16 is illness caused by sin, moral suffering, an important category when seen in the light of what we know about psycho-somatic illness. The sick person will be saved/healed (*sozo*), will be raised up (*egeiro*), will be forgiven (*aphethesetai*) and will be healed (*iathete*). This is a holistic view of health and healing.

The Words Used For Healing In The New Testament

All these words carry the idea of *shalom*—healing towards eternal wholeness with full reconciliation, restoration and resurrection.

- *sozo* means saved from danger—from illness and disease as well as from dangerous situations and spiritual danger. It is used repeatedly in the gospels in relation to healing, usually in the phrase 'your faith has saved you' which can just as well be translated 'your faith has healed you.' Salvation and healing are held within the same word.

- *iaomai*, although directly related to healing in its secular use, also carries the sense of Jesus' wider ministry of spiritual restoration from a state of sin.

- *egeiro* means to awaken from sleep. In the gospels it was used of the sick rising up, being strengthened and standing up whole and also of resurrection.

- *therapeuo* is used a great deal for healing in Jesus' ministry (and in the commission to the disciples in Luke 10.9), whereas in secular and inter-testamental Greek it was more often used of service for the good of others.

- *apokathistemi* has the sense of restoration to an earlier condition. It was used of future restoration of Israel as well as of a sick person being restored to health.

- *anistemi* is used for rising up, whether from sleep, the sick-bed, or from death (in restoration of physical life or in resurrection).

So all these words carried a meaning wider than physical healing alone, and reflected the mission of Jesus and the church as being to the whole world at all levels, for full salvation and restoration.

In Jesus' healing ministry there is also a frequent element of being sent into the immediate future with fresh commitment. We could express this as healing *for* the future and as well as healing *from* a disease or situation. It is seen in different ways: 'go and show yourselves to the priests'; 'go and sin no more'; 'go and wash in the pool'; 'return home and tell how much God has done'; even 'go and say nothing.' Sometimes there is evidence of service following healing—Simon's mother-in-law serving a meal, or the blind beggar following Jesus. However, not all reacted to Jesus' ministry in a life-changing way. Several frustrated Jesus' ministry by disobeying his charge to stay quiet, and only one of the ten lepers turned and gave praise to God.

The Laying on of Hands and Anointing in the New Testament

Jesus used touch in blessing and healing. When Jesus blessed children by touch, he placed his hands on them. In healing he sometimes used the laying on of hands (suggesting a more formalized action), or he simply touched people, or he was touched by them as they came to him (see Table 1). The gospel texts use the plural for Jesus' laying on of hands (*epititheis tas cheiras*). So it seems most likely that Jesus used both hands in his ministry, and that this was the practice he passed to his disciples.

The gospels do not mention touch in relation to the disciples but it is evident in Acts. The term 'laying on of hands' is used in two out of the possible six instances involving touch in Acts, by Ananaias for Saul's blindness (Acts 9.17–19) and by Paul in healing Publius' father from fever (Acts 28.7–10). The other instances of touch are not specifically laying on of hands (Acts 3.7, 14.19–20, 20.10), and 'extraordinary miracles by the hands of Paul' may be colloquial (Acts 19.11).

With regard to anointing, Jesus is the 'Christ' (the Anointed One) chosen by God for his purposes. The old order has passed away, but the roles of priest and king are fulfilled in Christ, and in us his church who are to be a royal priesthood and a holy nation (1 Peter 2.9). There is no explicit reference to Jesus anointing with oil. Whether this is because it is just not commented upon, or whether he did not use it, we do not know. He did use spittle in the healing of the blind man (John 9.6) and the deaf man with speech problems (Mark 7.33), and this was generally accepted as having medicinal properties similar to oil. Jesus also referred to oil in the story of the good Samaritan.

Anointing was not specifically part of Christ's command to the disciples in Mark 6.7–13, but it is clear that prayer and anointing in his name carried his authority, for many were healed. And in the letter of James there is a clear injunction to pray over a sick person and anoint with oil (James 5.14). Even if Jesus' command is not explicit, both the laying on of hands and anointing have strong biblical precedent.

The Implications of the Biblical Evidence

The Bible leads us to ministry that expresses God's love and saving grace in its fullest sense, proclaims God's kingdom and future hope, and demonstrates God's power and Christ's victory.

Wholeness is more a biblical expectation than a narrow understanding of healing as physical relief of symptoms or cure of the cause of them, although this also takes place. We relate to God and to his world around us at many levels—physically, spiritually, socially, emotionally, psychologically, and environmentally, and God wills our *shalom* with him, within ourselves, and with family, community, society, and creation. When any area is out of sorts, out of harmony with God and his will, then dis-ease results. So prayer for wholeness involves prayer that can encompass this range, and be open to God being at work in any area. In the Old Testament we see the need for this *shalom* in the context of a covenantal relationship, and in the New Testament we see it worked out in the ministry of Jesus and the early church in the establishing of God's kingdom.

When any area is out of sorts, out of harmony with God and his will, then dis-ease results

There is clear biblical evidence of Jesus using touch, the laying on of hands and anointing with spittle, and of the early church using touch, the laying on of hands and anointing with oil. The practice varied and there are no clear patterns and few explicit instructions (with James 5 being the clearest).

Table 1: Touch in the Ministry of Jesus

Jesus using the laying on of hands

			Word root for the healing
Mk 6.5	A few healings only (because of unbelief)	He laid his hands on a few sick people and healed them	*therapeuo*
Lk 4.40–41	Those who were sick	He laid his hands on every one of them and healed them	*therapeuo*
Mk 8.22–26	Blind man at Bethsaida	The people begged Jesus to touch him, Jesus spat on his eyes, and laid hands on him twice	*emblepo* (see clearly)
Lk 13.10–17	Woman bent over with spirit of infirmity	Jesus laid hands on her	*sozo*

Jesus touched the sufferer

Mk 1.29–31 Mt 8.14–15 Lk 4.38–39	Peter's mother-in-law	He took her by the hand; touched her hand; he stood over her and rebuked the fever	*egeiro*
Mk 1.40–45 Mt 8.1–4 Lk 5.12–14	Cleansing of a leper	He stretched out and touched him	*katharizo* (clean)
Mk 5.21–43 Mt 9.18–26 Lk 8.40–56	Jairus' daughter	Took her by the hand and she rose	*anistemi*
Mt 9.27–31	Two blind men	Jesus touched their eyes	*anoigo* (open)
Jn 9.1–41	Man born blind	Made clay of spittle, and anointed his eyes	*anablepo* (see again)
Lk 7.1 1–17	Widow's son at Nain	Touched the bier, and told him to rise	*egeiro*
Mk 7.32–37	Deaf man with speech impediment	Put his fingers in the man's ears, spat, and touched his tongue	*anoigo* (open) *luo* (loosen)
Mt 20.29–34	Two blind men	Jesus touched their eyes	*anablepo* (see again)
Lk 22.51	The slave's ear	Jesus touched his ear and healed him	*iaomai*

The sufferer touched Jesus

Mk 3.10	People were healed	'And all the crowd sought to touch him for power came forth from him and healed them all'	*therapeuo*
Mk 5.25–34 Mt 9.20–22 Lk 8.43–48	Woman with haemorrhage	She touched his garment	*sozo* and *laomai*
Mt 14.34–36 Mk 6.53–56	Healings at Genesaret	Whoever touched the fringe of his garment was made well	*dia-sozo*

Jesus never touched those who were demonized (Mk 5.1–20; Mt 8.28–32; Lk 4.33–37; Mt 9.32–33) or in the rebuking of a demon (Mk 9.14– 29; Mt 17.14–21; Lk 9.37–43)

Honesty and Hope

Whilst affirming the hope of wholeness and healing, because of the nature, power and love of God, we are also aware of the real pain, brokenness and distress that many face. Brokenness as well as wholeness is part of the gospel story, epitomized in Christ's brokenness on the cross before resurrection and ascension. Christ did not avoid pain and death. He understands our human frailty and vulnerability, and came into the world to be part of it as well as to change it.

Total physical health was not invariably the expectation or the experience of either Jesus or the early church. Jesus never refused any who came to him, but there were instances when he did not heal due to unbelief (Matthew 13.58) or healed selectively such as at the Pool of Bethsaida (John 5). Paul refers to the illness of Timothy (1Timothy 5.23), Trophimus (2 Timothy 4.20), Epaphroditus (Philippians 2.25–30) and his own 'thorn in the flesh' (2 Cor 12.7f)—although this may not have been a physical ailment. Paul taught that true wholeness will not come until the 'perishable puts on the imperishable, and the mortal puts on immortality' (1 Cor 15.42–57) and in the meantime we wait with eager longing (Romans 8.18–25). Death is 'the last enemy to be destroyed' (1 Cor 15.26) and will come to each of us, though Paul reminds us that not even death can separate us from the love of God in Christ Jesus (Rom 8.38).

He came into the world to be part of our frailty and vulnerability as well as to change it

Similarly sin and evil are still a reality, as Christ's victory is complete but not yet fully consummated. We can suffer as victims of sin—either our own, or that of others. However, Jesus did not endorse a simplistic view of a person's illness being a direct consequence of that person's sin. On occasions it was forgiveness that a person required, as with the paralysed man, but at other times he made it clear that sin was not an underlying cause, as with the man born blind. When there is a clear case of personal sin, then the ministry of reconciliation assures us of God's forgiveness and mercy through Christ, bringing inner peace and healing. But frequently we are on the receiving end of the sin of others. Sometimes the effects of sin are so deeply ingrained that it is hard to identify the cause and effect. We may be suffering from the collective sins of past generations, such as pollution, or unwise agricultural, industrial or economic policies. Endemic social sins such as prejudice, oppression or undermining of personal value, may not be ours to repent of.

Our ministry may need to be that of drawing close to those who suffer, with assurance of God's love and his presence, as they go through their dark places, or to accept and prepare for death with assurance of eternal life.

3 The Historical Background

After the time of the apostles the laying on of hands in ministry to the sick became formalized and practised widely.

The writings of Eusebius of Caesarea, Clement of Alexandria, and Irenaeus all refer to it with the expectation of healing as a result. By the third century there appears to be a variety of practice, from blessing followed by signing the affected part with the cross, to full laying on of hands with anointing, with which the bishop was charged in the Canons of Hippolytus. The laying on of hands was also an important part of the rite of reconciliation. The Council of Carthage in 256 refers to it for reconciliation of a penitent but this led to a controversy between Carthage and Rome. It was retained, until recent times, only in the form of raising the right hand in absolution.

Up until the beginning of the ninth century anointing was used for the sick, and the ministry was not restricted to the clergy. A biblical understanding of wholeness is reflected in many of the liturgical sources, and there are accounts of the laying on of hands and healing. The problem in assessing the historical accuracy of such reports is the hagiography that surrounds them.

Healing became the exceptional miracle associated with sainthood

Gradually healing became the exceptional miracle associated with sainthood, rather than the common practice of the church as a whole. General church ministry tended to relate to the soul rather than the body. From the ninth century onwards the liturgical history reflects a loss of the early church's confidence and a withdrawal from formal ministry to the sick. Loving care seemed to replace an expectation of healing through prayer. There was a developing emphasis on anointing, involving laying on of hands, used as preparation for death rather than for healing. It was administered by priests, gradually excluding the laity from this ministry. So by the Middle Ages it was practised as *extreme unction* and conflated with the rites of penance and final communion (*viaticum*). This gave rise to controversy at the Reformation.

The acceptance of only the two sacraments of Baptism and Communion automatically denied the sacramental value of laying on of hands or anointing. The Reformers did not accept the evidence of Mark 6 as a basis for a rite for healing. Bucer said 'this rite...has been introduced by a distorted imitation of an apostolic act, of whose imitation the ministers have manifestly neither a mandate nor a faculty,'[2] and that the Mark 6 passage showed that the apostles used oil but that this still did not constitute an adequate scriptural basis of a rite. He condemned the superstition surrounding it and called for its abolition. He saw Communion as being sufficient provision, for it was this 'by which the sick may be abundantly strengthened in health.' Calvin called it 'a mere hypocritical stage play.' Luther, in a letter to a pastor, advised him to lay on hands with two or three good men, but this instruction was not reflected in services for the sick, even though he had seen dramatic healing following ministry.

The collective memory of the misuse and abuse of anointing meant the C of E was reluctant to use it

In England an attempt to reintroduce anointing for the sick with prayers for recovery was its inclusion in the Bishops' Book of 1537, written by a committee of bishops and scholars. Their positive encouragement to use oil as a sacrament of healing was based on their belief that Mark 6 and James 5 were an adequate scriptural basis for the practice. But, despite this view, the collective memory of the misuse and abuse of the sacrament of unction meant the Church in England was reluctant to use it.

The 1549 *Prayer Book* provided for anointing the sick, but the ministry laid down in the 1552 *Prayer Book* took the form of only a visitation to the sick which majored on confession of sin. The 1662 *Prayer Book* repeated this same emphasis on the need for repentance and confession, seeing illness as a matter of God's correction, and for the building of faith and patience. As such it is to be submitted to with thanks, and with a sense of sharing in Christ's suffering for future benefit. There was no provision for anointing, no laying on of hands, and no expectation of healing. This was the only authorized service in general use in the Church of England for many years,[3] and unction remained a rite in the Roman church, but for the dying only.

The Eighteenth Century Onwards

In the eighteenth century the Non-jurors, in their concern to return to early practices of the church, reintroduced a service for the visitation of the sick, including unction, for recovery and not *in extremis*. In their liturgy of 1718 they include the laying on of hands during absolution, and in 1734 during prayer for the sick person, but much controversy surrounded both.

In the nineteenth century the Tractarian Movement taught that the church was endowed with 'the power of dispensing grace through rites of its own appointing,' and wanted to reintroduce and incorporate many practices then neglected. Forbes, Pye and Grueber took up the point and urged the restoration of unction, for although its original meaning had become distorted, they felt this was no excuse for its neglect. Forbes deplored the loss of a 'distinctly spiritual practice,' and Pye said it was 'very dangerous to leave [it] undone.'

It was not until the 1930s that the Church of England officially approved services for anointing and laying on of hands. There had been three notable developments that had led to a renewed awareness of the ministry—healing that accompanied revival, a recovery of the sacramental ministry towards healing amongst Anglo-Catholics, and the influential ministry of some key high-profile individuals. A committee appointed by the 1920 Lambeth Conference said in their report in 1924:

> These rites have scriptural authority and are sacramental in the sense that a blessing is sought and received through the performance of outward and visible actions. The motive with which they are used is the dedication of the bodily life of the patient to God's will.

The acceptance of the report was followed by the House of Convocation approving services for their administration in 1935 at Canterbury, and 1936 at York. In 1944 The Churches' Council for Health and Healing was inaugurated as an ecumenical body, and in 1953 an Archbishop's Commission was set up that reported in 1958. Over the following twenty years there were further developments within the ministry of healing in all areas of church. However, revised liturgical provision in the Church of England was not ready for the *1980 Alternative Service Book*. A supplementary set of services was later authorized in 1983 (*Ministry to the Sick*), which provided a comprehensive liturgy for use with the sick, including anointing and the laying on of hands.

In the last two decades there has been a growing acceptance of the validity of praying for wholeness and healing

In the last two decades there has been a growing acceptance of the validity of praying for wholeness and healing. Both renewal and increased confidence in this ministry has led all parts of the church to encourage the development of both formal and informal prayer, with the laying on of hands and anointing with oil, establishing patterns that are appropriate for the context and church tradition of the situation. God's love and power has been in evidence through a variety of styles of ministry, and there has been greater openness to the insights gained in different traditions. The latest report (*A Time to Heal*—see note 1) and the CW services reflect this in the Church of England.

What Happens When We Lay On Hands and Anoint?

4

Physical Aspect

Touch is a physical act which God uses to bless us at different levels of our experience and need. Theories concerning pain and pain control have implications for the ministry of the laying on of hands. Information going from the body to the brain about noxious stimuli is subject to controlling and modulating influences. Touch plays a part in the modulation at a local level. The nerve fibres which transmit information about touch are of a type which can 'close' the pain gate, that is, modulate perception of pain at a local level. These fibres can be stimulated by the mechanical effect of touch as the skin tissue is held, or moved, rubbed or pressed. This is one influence in an extremely complex process, but it is an important one. It is why we will often rub a sore spot, and why a cuddle will alleviate the sense of pain after being hurt. Thus, although the laying on of hands is only very light touch, there is nevertheless a physical contact which can in itself contribute to pain relief.

Psychological Aspect

Touch can transcend barriers. Barriers of fear, lack of trust, difficulty in communicating our needs, or difficulty in receiving assurance of acceptance and forgiveness, can be overcome in the simple act of touch. In communicating the loving acceptance of the one suffering, by the Lord and by other people, this ministry can lessen depression, rejection feelings, or even some obsessions. It may divert attention, new priorities of thought can develop, and perceptions can alter. Consequently it can affect emotional, social, or psychological needs with physical implications for our body systems.

Because the brain can modulate pain perception, pain is now accepted as a psychological or even emotional experience as much as a physical one. The quality and intensity of pain can be affected by the person's past history, the significance of the pain experience to their life, and the cultural and environmental background. The state of mind at the time, including thoughts, preoccupations, anxieties, hopes and fears also affects pain perception. The effect that such influences have on pain can either lessen it (as in heroic acts of bravery) or increase it (as in periods of depression). The laying on of hands can have an effect in many of these areas.

Spiritual Aspect

The laying on of hands is first and foremost the touch of the Lord. The spiritual aspect of what is happening is profound, as healing is the bringing of wholeness in positive spiritual terms leading towards eternal life, rather than just the negation of disease (although it can be this also). The healing that takes place happens as Christ's love and power works within the whole life of the person receiving ministry.

There are two gospel passages which explicitly introduce the idea of transference of power in a tangible sense associated with healing. In the healing of the woman with a haemorrhage Jesus felt power go out of him (Mark 5.25–34) and Luke tells of the crowds seeking to touch Jesus for 'power came forth from him and he healed them all' (Luke 6.19). Acts also talks of the Holy Spirit's power within the disciples almost as if it were a commodity— 'You will receive power when the Holy Spirit comes upon you' (Acts 1.8) —and Stephen is described as full of grace and power (Acts 6.8). Any power is, of course, of God (2 Corinthians 4.7) and not in any sense ours. We need to distinguish Christian ministry from other approaches that talk of energy transfer. By the power of the Holy Spirit it is Christ's touch which brings all the fullness of spiritual blessing which is his to give. It is therefore Christ ministering, and not a passing on of an anonymous power or force. For a minister to be 'a channel' for God's love and power, there first has to be a personal opening up to that love and to his Spirit, so that Christ may work through us to his purpose, and show his love to others through us.

Sacramental Aspect

There is value in the laying on of hands and anointing as outward signs of what God is doing within, and as tangible expressions of Christ's touch at the deepest levels. Despite the abuses evident in history, there is an important role to be played by actions through which God's grace can be mediated in the context of the ministry of his church. The outward activity symbolizes an encounter with God and sets a seal upon what is happening inwardly, thereby in itself contributing to that encounter.

Communion is also important as the sacrament which brings us to a point of meeting with God's mercy and grace in Christ. The service of Holy Communion declares God's saving love and Christ's saving death, and therefore has great importance in terms of forgiveness and wholeness. The sacramental aspect of the healing ministry should therefore be recognized and encouraged both in the centrality of Communion and in the use of these outward expressions of Christ's ministry within.

Some Notes On Practice 5

Preparation

Prayer should surround the ministry of healing. Preparation by those ministering begins well before the service in personal prayer, quiet openness to God's Spirit, and ensuring that they arrive without too many distractions or too much busyness in activity or thought. It is important to have some corporate time of prayer for those ministering, and preferably some time praying together for those ministering in pairs. Preparation by those receiving ministry may include counselling and self-examination prior to confession, as well as spending time drawing close to the Lord, so that Christ is at the very centre of all that takes place. However, those who are ill or incapacitated may just need encouragement to rest and be peaceful, becoming aware of Christ's love for them, without placing any demands upon them.

The Laying on of Hands

As in Jesus' ministry touching someone can be either a specific laying on of hands, or something more informal. The circumstances may dictate which approach is used.

The laying on of hands involves placing hands on the head, or one hand on the head and the other on neck or shoulders, or a combination of these if two are ministering. The touch is light and should not feel like an oppressive pressure to the recipient. Some advocate a hand lightly placed on the chest when an emotional problem is expressed (with obvious precautions to ensure women minister to women in this case). Others suggest placing a hand wherever the symptom is manifested, again with sensitivity and wisdom. Those ministering who find that they shake when they pray need to be careful not to alarm the one receiving ministry, or to draw attention to themselves distracting from the important focus of prayer. Variations in practice occur quite frequently.

The less formal use of touch is usually prayer whilst holding hands, or with an arm round the shoulder. Because of the informal nature this can be less intimidating than the laying on of hands. However, it can also be more subject to misinterpretation as it is more personal. Permission should be asked before assuming that touch is acceptable when ministering.

Some charismatic ministers do not actually touch whilst praying but hold the hand a few inches away from the person. This is mainly done to avoid accusations of pushing someone over if they fall, but it loses some of the benefits of touch.

There is no theological reason why any Christian cannot use the laying on of hands. It is, after all, only a natural action accompanying intercession. However, in a service there is an expectation that those ministering have the trust and authority of the church for this ministry, and they should therefore be at least locally approved and trained.

> ### Common Worship Words of Administration for the Laying on of Hands
>
> In the name of Christ and trusting in his might alone,
> receive Christ's healing touch to make you whole.
>
> May Christ bring you wholeness of body, mind and spirit,
> deliver you from every evil, and give you his peace. Amen.

Anointing With Oil

Many involved in the healing ministry hold anointing to be of a different nature to the laying on of hands, as a profound act, requiring thorough preparation with counselling and serious reflection and confession prior to ministry. It is seen as applicable to those with deep illnesses, or people who are organically 'sick' with their illness. Because of the element of dedication and consecration, anointing is used not only for healing but also for deliverance (not exorcism), for protection, at a time of crisis, or for equipping for a particular task. Such anointing should be done in response to clear direction from the Lord that it is right to do so, or when someone asks for it specifically. However, as anointing is an accessible and helpful support to prayer ministry, there are others who feel it should be more readily available.

It is recommended that a prayer of thanksgiving is at the heart of the rite

Canon B37 governs the practice of anointing in the Church of England. This says that the oil should be pure olive oil. It can be consecrated by the Bishop at the service or on a previous occasion (traditionally this is done on Maundy Thursday) or by the presiding priest. In the notes to the Celebration of Wholeness and Healing, it is recommended that the consecration is done at the service to ensure there is enough oil, and that a prayer of thanksgiving is put at the heart of the rite. CW provides a form for this prayer.

Ideally anointing is administered, as in James, by the elders of the church gathered around the sick person. CW expects the oil to be administered by the presiding priest, but allows delegation to 'other ministers authorized for this ministry under Canon B37.' This phrase has been taken by some to be a little ambiguous. In some churches the ministry has become such a natural and accepted part of church life that it is practised widely and by a large number of people. This is not how it has been envisaged officially because of the desire to ensure appropriate use and avoid abuse.

Anointing involves making the sign of the cross on the forehead and occasionally on the hands. Oil is an exceptionally messy element. It easily runs everywhere, and is quite sticky and damaging to clothes. The easiest way to control it is to put some into a small container with cotton wool, making sure that there is enough wool to absorb most of the oil. Holding the container firmly, dip the pad of the thumb into the oil. The thumb is then used to make the sign of the cross.

There are those who feel the symbolism is clearer when the oil is used more liberally, and allowed to run down the face or through the hair, as a sign of the liberality of God's love. This has practical implications which must be addressed, otherwise it becomes a distraction to the primary focus of the ministry—the encounter with, and touch of, Christ.

Common Worship Words of Administration when Using Oil

N, I anoint you in the name of God who gives you life.
Receive Christ's forgiveness, his healing and his love.

May the Father of our Lord Jesus Christ, grant you the riches of his grace, his wholeness and his peace. Amen.

Reaction to Ministry

Reactions to ministry vary considerably and can include:

- silent acceptance of Christ's touch;
- emotional release in tears of intense sorrow, joy, or laughter;
- physical manifestations such as shaking, swaying, falling, vibration;
- relief of physical symptoms or correction of physical disabilities;
- sensations such as heat, power, electric shock, light, or tingling;
- feelings of wonder, or a deep sense of peace or purpose;
- assurance of the promise of soon being taken to be with God;
- disappointment if nothing is felt or nothing apparently happens.

More extreme reactions have been frequent, especially at times of revival. Recently the 'Third Wave' of renewal and the 'Toronto Blessing' have been accompanied with some dramatic manifestations such as uncontrollable movement, loud noises or shouts, intense laughter or even animal sounds. Concern has been expressed at some of these manifestations. At times they will be signs of God's deep and mysterious work in a person's life. However, they should not be used as a measure of what God is doing inwardly, nor should they be sought for their own sake. Rather than focus on the manifestations it is more helpful to accept that such things may or may not happen, and are most probably just ways of expressing release and freedom.

Dealing with Reaction

Part of training for ministry should include preparation for possible reactions and openness to how God may meet a person. By being aware that different reactions can occur, shock or surprise will not translate into judgement or overreaction.

Practical preparation needs to be made to cope with some of the possible reactions. For example it is desirable:

- To have one person (or more) present who will care for the person receiving ministry: to catch them if they fall and especially to protect their head; to ensure their modesty if they are overcome and are not aware of their clothing; to be with them when they become aware of how they have reacted to ministry to give them affirmation, help, encouragement, or just practical help to walk back to their seat.

- To make provision for those who may be unable to return home without help. For example someone who drove to the service may be very 'high' afterwards, and may need time to settle or to be taken home.

- To have at least one minister present who has the expertise or experience to cope with someone who has severe problems, extreme reaction, or demonic influence. This may not need to be dealt with at the time, but there should be arrangements in place to care for that person until more extensive and specialist ministry can take place.

- To have information available on how to receive further help. This is especially important in services where those receiving ministry are not regular or known members of the congregation.

Different Contexts and Styles of Ministry

6

Common Worship Provision

The CW services provide for a variety of contexts: *A Celebration of Wholeness and Healing*, with or without Holy Communion (primarily provided for larger services such as a diocesan or deanery occasion); *The Laying on of Hands and Anointing* in the context of Holy Communion (for regular church use); *Prayer for individuals in Public Worship* (for regular ministry in churches); *Ministry to the Sick*; and a collection of prayers as a resource. Only aspects relating to the ministry of the laying on of hands and anointing are considered here.[4]

Ministry Within the Context of Holy Communion

In the *Celebration of Wholeness and Healing*, and in the basic pattern offered for parish ministry, the ministry time is separated from the distribution of Communion. This gives two clear focal points: the ministry of the laying on of hands and anointing which is directed at our needs; and Communion which is focused more specifically on Christ. This pattern allows an extended time of ministry, and freedom to use either formal or informal prayer. Only those who wish to receive ministry will come forward and the ministry teams can be placed so that privacy is respected.

The healing work of Christ is supremely expressed in his death and resurrection

The pattern of receiving the laying on of hands at the time of the communion distribution is also allowed. For practical reasons this is usually done with a short formal prayer. Usually the bread is given to the communicant, followed by prayer for those who wish to receive it, and then the administration of wine. The prayer for healing is seen to be part of the healing work of Christ supremely expressed in his death and resurrection. There is no embarrassment about coming for prayer, as it is part of coming for Communion along with most of the congregation.

Ministry in the Context of Other Services

The main advantage of non-communion services is their inclusive nature for those who are not regular churchgoers. If healing is one of the signs of the kingdom then introduction to Christ through services with a focus on prayer for healing is not out of place. These services can also be used in an evening when Communion has already been celebrated, and for ecumenical occasions. They are flexible and have fewer time restraints. The advantage of focusing on the saving work of Christ that Communion brings is lost, but that can be put into other parts of the service. The *Celebration for Wholeness and Healing* marks the Liturgy of the Sacrament as optional.

Ministry Within Regular Services

This approach is to be commended, especially when the service is one of Holy Communion. Wholeness and healing will then be seen to be part of the mainstream ministry of the church and part of the whole gospel message. Those being prayed for will be surrounded by the regular worshipping body of Christ in that place and it will give real expression to the family of God and his kingdom. Preparation, counselling and prayer support before the service, as well as follow-up care and prayer after ministry, can all be carefully and lovingly practised. The usual minister and known brothers and sisters in Christ will be the ones administering Christ's touch. They will continue to be there to encourage if there is disappointment, or to rejoice if answer to prayer is more immediately obvious. Teaching can be given over a period of time, and the purpose of the service, method of ministry, and theological and spiritual aspects can be made clear, avoiding wrong attitudes or abuse of ministry.

Wholeness and healing will then be seen to be part of the whole gospel message

Regular ministry, handled sensitively, means that there are frequent and open opportunities for anyone in the congregation to come to the Father, with the praying community, as a natural extension of worship and intercession.

Ministry in Home and Hospital

Small services of healing in the home or hospital are perhaps the closest parallel we have here with James' instruction to call for the elders to come and pray. The elders of the church directly express the love and concern of the fellowship, and in this context the laying on of hands and anointing can be a particular point of communication of love. Holy Communion in hospital is normally the duty of the hospital chaplain and he or she should be consulted when deciding on how to minister to a parishioner in hospital. Provision for this ministry in CW gives a variety of material to suit different occasions.[5]

Approaches to the Time of Ministry

There is no one correct method of ministry. The approach used will need to arise and develop from the local situation. This means having the courage to adopt practices that are right for the fellowship, rather than importing a whole 'package' approach to such ministry.

a) Formal

Ministry as a formal act accompanied by a short set prayer, in either a public service or a private situation.

Advantages: It uses the symbolism of the laying on of hands and anointing to convey the touch of the Lord and its simplicity makes it very meaningful. Paradoxically this is the most unlimited approach. An all-encompassing prayer, which asks God to touch at all levels of a person's life, leaves all in his hands. The subsequent thoughts and prayers are entirely between that person and the Lord. There is therefore less chance of the minister's own personality influencing the ministry. It is less probing and therefore more private, accessible to the hesitant and takes less time.

Disadvantages: The ministry can feel a bit impersonal and there is no opportunity for the expression of the gifts of discernment and knowledge. People cannot mention specific matters for prayer.

b) Informal Prayer in a Formal Setting

A freer form of prayer within a formal service.

Advantages: This is a more personal approach allowing specific requests for prayer. It gives scope for prayer by both the one coming with need and those designated to minister, and for the guidance of the Holy Spirit in how to pray and in the use of spiritual gifts. There is an opportunity for brief conversation to identify further areas of pain or to feed back thoughts and trigger questions which may 'unlock' an area of pain, sin or memory. In conjunction with further counselling and continued ministry within a caring, sensitive community, it can bring great blessing.

Disadvantages: Within worship, especially if there is a time restraint, there is a practical difficulty of time and order. Those coming up later may get cut short, or people may have to sit through very long ministry times. Prayer can turn into a counselling session, or areas can be explored at insufficient depth leaving unfinished business. Without further ministry this can be harmful.

c) Informal Prayer in an Informal Setting

The most natural pattern in a home or private situation, but also possible within services.

i) Ministry-time at the end of the service
This, in effect, removes it from the liturgical setting, and thereby allows limitless time.

Advantages: No restrictions, and no pressures.
Disadvantages: It separates ministry from worship, jeopardizing the sense of the whole body undergirding the ministry in prayer, especially if people begin to chatter or drift away.

ii) Setting aside a room for the ministry, or a more private place in the church, to which people are taken when they come forward, or to which they are invited to go if they want prayer

Advantages: No restrictions on time, and privacy for the ministry.
Disadvantages: A daunting journey into the unknown is created for those who are timid about going forward. There can be a feeling of separation from what everyone else is experiencing, and a lack prayer support for the ministry as the rest of the service goes on—'out of sight, out of mind.'

iii) The whole congregation being involved in a time of generalized ministry.
As people sense the touch of the Lord on someone near them they pray in support of the Lord's activity. This is reactive rather than proactive prayer, and acknowledges the work of God that is already going on. This happens where there is awareness of what God is doing and opportunity for the Holy Spirit to minister either in a time set apart for this, or by a willingness to stop the expected order of service for it to happen.

Advantages: The whole body of Christ is involved in the experience of God moving among them to touch and to heal. There is openness to what God wishes to do, without prayer which seeks to direct what he does.

Disadvantages: The temptation is to intervene and offer inappropriate ministry, particularly by the immature or untrained.

d) Public Prayer
Formal laying on of hands and anointing, with additional extempore prayer, for each person in turn, in front of the congregation. This ministry is very focused and highly public. It involves preparation that includes declaration of desire to receive prayer, thought about what words of testimony and information will be given publicly, counselling, and support.

Advantages: There is a strong element of ownership by all concerned. This is prayer of the local church that gives the individual a sense of being loved and supported by the whole community.

Disadvantages: Its public nature will be off-putting for some, and it will be limited by this and the number of people for whom it is practical to pray.

Deciding What To Pray

7

Pray With a Biblical View of Health. Being aware of the holistic nature of God's dealings with us should affect our approach to what we pray.

Pray According To God's Own Nature. Jesus taught his disciples to pray 'Your Kingdom come, your will be done.' Deepening our knowledge of God, and our relationship with him, helps protect against praying for things that cannot be God's will.

Pray in the Name of Christ. The healing of the lame man at Gate Beautiful testifies to the reality and power of Jesus at work in and through his church, in his name (Acts 3–4). It is Christ who ministers, and it is in his name that we share in this work.

Pray in the Spirit. Allowing the Spirit to direct our praying may include giving us a gift of knowledge, or discernment, or wisdom (among others), or guiding our thoughts very specifically for the needs of the situation. Praying in tongues, preferably silently, can be of help when we are unsure of what to pray—as the Holy Spirit 'helps us in our weakness' or even takes over the prayer altogether in 'sighs too deep for words' (Romans 8.26–27).

Pray in Line With God's Activity. Jesus said that his ministry was to do what he saw the Father doing (John 5.19). Similarly our ministry is to work with what God is doing in a person's life, so we need to be attentive to what this is, and open to what it might be.

Pray As We Have Been Taught. The Lord's Prayer models coming to our heavenly Father in worship and dependence, wanting his kingdom and his will to prevail as we make our request, aware of our need for his grace in forgiveness, guidance and protection. Jesus's repeated instruction to the disciples in John 14 –16 to ask for what they want in Christ's name is linked to being united with Christ. If we have Christ and his word in us then we will ask for things that bring glory to the Father, and that will work towards his kingdom and the bearing of fruit that will last.

Pray with Childlike Faith And Humility. Our relationship with God is as children with a loving heavenly Father. Stepping out in simple, humble faith is a sound basis for ministry—not eloquence, or intellectual and theological athleticism, or sainthood! A childlike trust and faith is a good starting point.

Offer Person-centred Prayer. A helpful way to approach prayer ministry[6] is to enable the verbalizing of prayer by the one expressing need. This encourages a direct and honest prayer to God, free from the dangers of the misinterpretation, inaccuracy and personal agenda of those appointed to share in the ministry. Giving permission and space to allow the person to explore their own feelings towards their situation and towards God, fosters a deeper personal encounter, and more ownership of the ministry.

Pray 'Between the Lines.' The initial prayer request may not always reveal the most important factor in the situation. Careful listening and loving attentiveness may bring out things that are less obvious but of great importance. We need to listen to the individual, and in our listening pray for God's guidance to discern what the focus of ministry should be. Sometimes it is better to pray in silence, and to hold areas of concern in our own prayer, without voicing them, so that the person with whom we are praying is not overwhelmed or distracted by our words, or the noise or content of our praying. It helps to pray with eyes open, as we can be more attentive to reactions, to body language, and to sensing God's work in the person for whom we pray.

8 Cautions and Precautions[7]

The Negative Aspects of Touch
Touching is subject to social norms and a whole range of interpretation, and can carry negative as well as positive messages. Socially acceptable forms of touch vary in different societies. In Britain we are generally over-anxious about the implications of casual touch (especially between male and female), and guard our 'personal space' to secure our privacy. Jouard's research into cultural patterns of touch tells of the number of times touch was involved in a conversation between two people in a café.[8] In Puerto Rico two people touched 180 times per hour and in London not at all!

However, increased informality, relaxation of social norms, and the multicultural nature of many of our cities now make for a more complicated picture. Each person who receives ministry is likely to understand physical touch in a different way. It is easy to assume that a person would be happy to receive the laying on of hands, but this should not be taken for granted. It may be that the person receiving ministry is uncomfortable at being touched. To avoid misunderstandings it is necessary to be extremely sensitive to any signs of embarrassment or disquiet in the one to be prayed with, and to stress in every situation that it is the touch of *the Lord*, and the stretching forth of *his* hand, that is taking place and that brings healing.

Caution is needed over the positioning of hands and the gender and approach of those ministering. Very heavy touch can also be alarming and counterproductive, and can feel oppressive—especially if administered to the crown of the head.

Confidentiality
Respecting confidentiality is crucial. If the minister cannot be trusted to maintain confidentiality, there is a real barrier to honest and effective prayer. The content of the prayer must remain strictly a matter between the person for whom prayer is made and Christ. Anyone ministering is a facilitator and bystander to an intimate encounter. It is a privileged and responsible place to be and must not be abused. Sometimes there is a burden to be carried by those ministering, when party to distressing information or deep concern. If this becomes too weighty to carry it may be necessary to seek permission from the person with whom you prayed to share it with someone trustworthy, such as the minister of the church. This must be done with care, and not shared unless such permission is given. The spouse of someone who ministers will need to come to terms with the fact that there will be areas of concern from which they are excluded. It is not always easy to deal with this.

Take-over and Disabling
Pray 'with' rather than pray 'for.' We draw alongside one another in intercession when we pray with someone—we are not engaged as professionals praying instead of them. Do not disable the prayer of others by assuming a dominant or patronizing air. Fostering and enabling their relationship with God is as important as any other aspect of the ministry. They need to be enabled to relate directly to God in their situation, not become dependent on those who minister or encouraged to abdicate responsibility for their own life or healing. This ministry is not a place to exercise power or control.

Slipping into a Counselling Session
There is a difference between the ministry of healing and counselling. In counselling 'empathy' is a necessary giving of oneself, and an entering into the situation and feelings of the client. In some instances, especially in an informal setting, ministry for healing can become more of a counselling session. Sympathy leading to empathy may well help the recipient, and there is a real place for Christian counselling. However, in the ministry of the laying

on of hands it is Christ's touch that we seek, and it is better to allow space for counselling in preparation or follow-up rather than at the time of prayer.

Self Projection

Know yourself, and your own needs and concerns. You are then more able to recognize when you are in danger of projecting these onto the person for whom you are praying.

The Danger of Loading Guilt

a) With Regard to Faith

There is no biblical evidence for saying that faith *on the part of the sufferer* is a pre-requisite for healing. Sometimes healing had the effect of facilitating or increasing faith; at other times healing was in response to or reward for faith. It is true that in Matthew 13.58 we are told Jesus could not do many works because of unbelief; but the blind man in John 9, the man at the pool in John 5, Legion in Mark 5, and the crippled beggar in Acts 3 were all healed without prior faith. Certainly faith is necessary, but it can be the faith of those praying or the church family as a whole. Loading guilt onto someone that they did not have enough faith to be healed is damaging and unbiblical.

b) With Regard to 'Blocking Healing'

A specific expectation on the part of those praying can tempt them to demand that the recipient responds in a particular way at the time of prayer. If there is apparently no response in their terms, it is all too easy for their disappointment to be turned to a guilt-inducing enquiry about what is 'blocking healing.' If there are underlying issues that need addressing it is for the Holy Spirit to do the convicting, in a way and at a time which God directs, and a period of counselling can help explore deeper areas alongside or in preparation for further ministry.

Guru Mentality and Personality Cults

There is a danger of 'solo' or 'guru' figures emerging within the local church which can take the focus away from the ministry being Christ's own touch. All ministry should be based in and flow from the church, recognizing it as Christ's body on earth. It is the church as a whole that is charged, equipped, and authorized to minister in his name by his Holy Spirit, not just gifted individuals.

Partnership with Medicine

God works through medicine alongside the prayer ministry of the church. A dismissive attitude towards medical care and medical treatment can put lives at risk, or do serious long-term damage. The encouragement to express faith by rejection of medical care or treatment is irresponsible.

Who Can Minister? 9

The Whole Church

Whether involved specifically or not, the whole congregation needs to take on the role of intercessors, so that the ministry is an expression of the praying, healing community by which it is backed. It also leads to a growing expectation of seeing God at work within their lives and the community.

Representatives of the Church

Authority to minister can be delegated to those who share in the church's leadership. Godly and spiritual men and women commissioned by the Bishop or incumbent (in the Church of England), or equivalent office in other churches, would seem to equate closely with the elders in James.

Those With a Ministry of Healing

God can give any of the various charismata (gifts) through the Holy Spirit to any believer, for the edification of the church, and the work of his kingdom. This can be a one-off instance, but some people are recognized and affirmed as having a *ministry of healing*—repeatedly used by God in this way.

There are some who appear to have a psychic ability to heal. Those who are involved in the healing ministry warn against the 'christianizing' of psychic phenomena in place of Christ's own touch in people's lives.

The Ordained Clergy

Ordained clergy represent the total ministry of Christ's body, and have the authority of their call and ordination to exercise the church's ministry (even if they themselves have no ministry of healing). They also hold responsibility for the devolved ministry within a congregation. Priests have authority to pronounce blessing, are responsible for presiding at Communion (with its healing effect) and are authorized to absolve and anoint.

Ministry Teams

A ministry team can include any of the people above, but the exact mix will depend on the local situation and needs consideration early in the process of establishing the ministry. A balance of gender, cultural groups and so on is needed. If the team are also the regular intercessors in the main service, this can de-mystify the ministry and underline its intercessory nature. The ministers become known, and this can make approach for ministry less daunting. It can also stop the team being seen as a spiritual élite. PCC approval and an appropriate structure of authority and accountability are important.

Ministering in pairs is supported by the principle of going out in twos (Mark 6.7 and Luke 10.1). It encourages people to learn and develop in ministry and can prevent individualism and personality cults. Someone new to ministry can learn from an experienced partner, and both can learn from the observations of the other. One partner is silent at any time and has the opportunity to be receptive to the promptings of the Spirit. Pairings should have an appropriate mix of male and female, lay and ordained, those with clear gifts and those with a representative role, or those chosen to reflect an ecumenical context, or varied tradition of the churches involved.

The building up of the team members in their faith is foundational

Training is vital. Essentially the ministry is about being open to God and so the encouraging and building up of the team members in their faith and their knowledge of God and his word, together with attentiveness to the Holy Spirit, is foundational. The techniques and practicalities are necessary, but not a replacement for this central pre-requisite.

Training must include ministering to one another. The team learns to understand vulnerability and what it feels like to be prayed with. The concept of 'the wounded healer' is helpful and the team's own lack of wholeness and need for Christ's touch will become evident. They also learn about issues of confidentiality, the importance of trust and sensitivity, and how to recognize and avoid inappropriate ministry.

A ministry group may become aware of any pain present in the church community. Sometimes it becomes a focal point for the dis-ease which is normally buried or passed over in superficiality. Such growing pains can be distressing to a new group, but if the issues are worked through the group can become an important part of God's healing work to the whole church family.

Those who minister need support individually and as a team. Being on the front-line of the spiritual life of the church, they are especially vulnerable. Exposure to spiritual warfare, hurt and pain can leave them drained, burdened, and open to spiritual attack. Debriefing is helpful (with a clear policy on dealing with confidences), enabling the handing of responsibility back to Christ himself. Ongoing training and regular meetings help to build trust and a supportive environment from which to minister.

The Church as a Healing Community

10

The church's healing ministry is to be expressed not only in its activities but in its very nature.

Jesus' teaching stressed the importance of community. We are to live in fellowship and to love and value one another and our neighbour. In his ministry we see Jesus incorporating the outcast and marginalized. Healing meant acceptance back into society for lepers and others who were healed. Sometimes they were told to return to the fellowship of their extended family, or restoration could entail community action as with Zacchaeus. All this has implications for the church's ministry. It is to be a healing community where *shalom* is to be evident.

Those engaged in ministry teams are only a small part of the picture. Much of the healing that goes on, that people need today in a loveless and fragmented society, will happen through love, acceptance, being included and being valued. A loving community can reverse the damage of society's values, pressures, abuse, and self-centredness, that crush the spirit, and turn a person whom God created as precious into someone who is powerless, demotivated, marginalized, hurt and suffering. Healing also happens through people growing in discipleship and discovering they too have gifts, discovering their worth and value in God's eyes.

We express this healing community in services, and articulate in it the liturgy, as well as in the social life of the local church. Praise and worship of God puts things into God's perspective. Confession and assurance of God's forgiveness brings a

The Church is to be a healing community where shalom is to be evident

new start. Sharing the peace expresses the acceptance and reconciliation that we have with one another in Christ. We welcome those who come to new life in baptism. We share in the eucharistic feast. We minister to one another in song and music, intercession, practical tasks, preaching, teaching and testimony, as well as in prayer ministry.

The ministry of wholeness and healing should stem from and lead into this healing community, the Body of Christ.

11 Resources

'Wholeness and Healing,' in *Common Worship: Pastoral Services* (The Archbishops' Council, Church House Publishing, 2000) pp 8–99

Colin Buchanan, *Services for Wholeness and Healing: The Common Worship Orders* (Grove Worship booklet W 161)

A Time to Heal: A Report for the House of Bishops on the Healing Ministry (The Archbishops' Council, Church House Publishing, 2000)

John Woolmer, *Healing and Deliverance* (Monarch, 1990)

Morris Maddocks, *The Christian Healing Ministry* (SPCK, 1981)

John Leach, *Developing Prayer Ministry* (Grove Renewal booklet R1)

Rosemary Green, *God's Catalyst* (Christina Press, 1997)

Roger Vaughan, *Saints Alive! Healing in the Church* (Anglican Renewal Ministries, 2002)

Charles Gusmer, *The Ministry of Healing in the Church of England* (Alcuin/SPCK, 1984)

Martin Dudley and Geoffrey Rowell, *The Oil of Gladness* (SPCK, 1993)

Notes

1 *A Time to Heal: A Report for the House of Bishops on the Healing Ministry*, and 'Wholeness and Healing,' pp 8–99 in *Common Worship: Pastoral Services*, both published for The Archbishops' Council 2000, Church House Publishing.
2 C Gusmer, *The Ministry of Healing in the Church of England*, p 71.
3 In several editions of the Prayer Book there were services of royal healing, known as 'Touching for the King's Evil.' These were very specific and related more to the status of a monarch than to the healing ministry of Christ's church. The tradition probably originated with Edward the Confessor, for the healing of scrofula, a form of tuberculosis. Many monarchs continued the practice, finally ending with Queen Anne in 1712. Charles II is said to have touched 92,107 people according to a study by one of the royal physicians, John Browne.
4 Detailed commentary for these services is given in Colin Buchanan, *Services for Wholeness and Healing: The Common Worship Orders* (Grove Worship booklet W 161).
5 See Carolyn Headley, *Home Communion—A Practical Guide* (Grove Worship booklet W 157).
6 See John Leach, *Person-centred Prayer Ministry* (Anglican Renewal Ministries, 2001).
7 See the excellent and comprehensive guidelines in the report *A Time to Heal*, Appendix 1.
8 S M Jouard (1966) 'An exploratory study of body accessibility' *Br J Soc Clin Psychol* 5, pp 221–231.